BASEBALL
SUPERSTARS
2019

JON RICHARDS

CARLTON
KiDS

THIS IS A CARLTON BOOK
Text, design, and illustration © Carlton Books
Limited 2019

This edition published in 2019 by Carlton Books
Limited, an imprint of the Carlton Publishing Group,
20 Mortimer Street, London W1T 3JW

Written by Jon Richards
Designed by Tall Tree Ltd

Special thanks to Tom Lambiase and
Matt Frederick

ISBN: 978-1-78312-407-7

Printed in China

CONTENTS

MLB 2018 SEASON

Get ready to meet the superstars of Major League Baseball (MLB)! Read about the **GREATEST SLUGGERS** and **PITCHERS,** find out who really shines in a **WORLD SERIES,** and discover who are the **PLAYERS TO WATCH** in the years to come. Get the lowdown on the **HOTTEST STARS** and then test your knowledge with our tricky quiz.

PLAYERS AND STATS

The player profiles will tell you everything you need to know. Find out how the superstars finished last season to see how their record compares with 2019. For each player, you can see their 2018 regular season stats and their career stats.

BATTING AND BASE RUNNING

AB	R	H	HR	RBI	SB	AVG	OBP	OPS
AT BAT	RUNS SCORED	HITS	HOME RUNS	RUNS BATTED IN	STOLEN BASES	BATTING AVERAGE	ON-BASE PERCENTAGE	ON-BASE PLUS SLUGGING

PITCHING

W	L	ERA	G	GS	SV	IP	SO	WHIP
WINS	LOSSES	EARNED RUNS AVERAGE	GAMES	STARTS	SAVES	INNINGS PITCHED	STRIKEOUTS	WALKS AND HITS PER INNINGS PITCHED

SUPERSTARS CRYSTAL BALL

What do you think will happen in 2019? Who will go all the way and win the World Series? Who will be voted MVP? Make your predictions below and see how many you get right when the season ends. Don't forget, NL stands for National League, and AL stands for American League!

	MY PREDICTION	WHAT HAPPENED
NL MOST VALUABLE PLAYER		
AL MOST VALUABLE PLAYER		
NL CY YOUNG AWARD		
AL CY YOUNG AWARD		
NL ROOKIE OF THE YEAR		
AL ROOKIE OF THE YEAR		
WORLD SERIES WINNER		

AARON JUDGE

THIS GUY is destined for greatness having spent his rookie season **SMASHING RECORDS** held by the likes of Babe Ruth and Joe DiMaggio. **STANDING AT 6'7"** and weighing in at more than **280 POUNDS,** Judge is one of the biggest players on the field. And with a **POWERFUL PLAYING STYLE,** he's really one player you can't miss.

NEW YORK YANKEES

RIGHT FIELDER

D.O.B: APRIL 26, 1992

MLB DEBUT: AUGUST 13, 2016

HEIGHT: 6'7"

WEIGHT: 282 LBS

THROWS: RIGHT

BATS: RIGHT

JUDGE
99

STAT ATTACK

	AB	R	H	HR	RBI	SB	AVG	OBP	OPS
2018 (REGULAR SEASON)	413	77	115	27	67	6	.278	.392	.919
MLB CAREER	1,039	215	284	83	191	15	.273	.398	.963

ALL-AROUND SCHOOL STAR

While at school at Linden High School, California, Judge excelled at football, basketball, and baseball. He set a school record for touchdowns with 17, led his basketball team in points per game with 18.2, and was part of a baseball team that made the California Interscholastic Federation divisional playoffs. Several colleges approached him to play football, including Notre Dame, Stanford, and UCLA, but his first love was baseball and even though the Oakland Athletics selected him in the 2018 MLB Draft, he chose to go to California State University in Fresno.

HARD HITTING

His first full rookie season in 2017 saw Judge set record after record. He belted 52 home runs, breaking Mark McGwire's previous record of 49. In doing so, he smashed Joe DiMaggio's Yankees rookie record, which had only been 29, and Babe Ruth's team record for the most home runs hit at home (scoring 33 to Ruth's 32). On the way, he also recorded the hardest hit ball with a measured exit velocity of 121.1 mph.

FROM COLLEGE TO MLB

Judge soon became a key part of the Fresno State Bulldogs team and during his junior year, he led the team in home runs, doubles, and RBIs. During his time with the Bulldogs, he was named to the all-conference team three times (twice in the Western Athletic Conference and once in the Mountain West after the Bulldogs changed their conference). In 2013, the Yankees picked Judge with the 32nd overall selection of the MLB Draft, but a torn leg muscle ruled him out for an entire season. After two seasons in minor league baseball, working his way through the divisions, he finally made his MLB debut against the Tampa Bay Rays in August 2016, and in his very first at-bat in the majors he hit a home run .

Judge is chased down by Mariners' second baseman Dee Gordon in a dash to third base during a game in June 2018.

>>>>> FAST FACT >>>>>

Before each game at Yankee Stadium, Judge performs a number of rituals including tossing 40 sunflower seeds into the grass behind home plate and saying a prayer.

NOLAN ARENADO

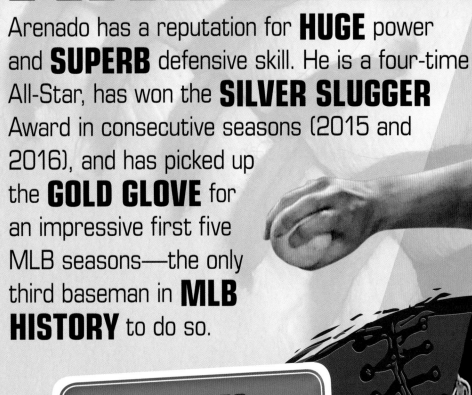

Arenado has a reputation for **HUGE** power and **SUPERB** defensive skill. He is a four-time All-Star, has won the **SILVER SLUGGER** Award in consecutive seasons (2015 and 2016), and has picked up the **GOLD GLOVE** for an impressive first five MLB seasons—the only third baseman in **MLB HISTORY** to do so.

COLORADO ROCKIES

THIRD BASEMAN

D.O.B: APRIL 16, 1991

MLB DEBUT: APRIL 28, 2013

HEIGHT: 6'2"

WEIGHT: 205 LBS

THROWS: RIGHT

BATS: RIGHT

ARENADO
28

STAT ATTACK

	AB	R	H	HR	RBI	SB	AVG	OBP	OPS
2018 (REGULAR SEASON)	590	104	175	38	110	2	.297	.374	.935
MLB CAREER	3,348	524	975	186	616	13	.291	.346	.886

ROCKIES ROOKIE

After playing for his high-school baseball team in Lake Forest, California, Arenado left college after the Colorado Rockies selected him in the second round of the 2009 draft. His time in the minors included an All-Star Futures selection in 2011 and 2012. After a red-hot start to the 2013 season with the Colorado Springs Sky Sox, he debuted for the Rockies on April 28. Picking up his first hit and a home run in his second game, he ended the season hitting .267 with 29 doubles and 10 homers in 133 games, and became the first rookie third baseman to win a Gold Glove since 1957.

ONE OF THE BEST

Arenado led the National League in homers and RBIs again in 2016, securing another All-Star place and repeating his Gold Glove and Silver Slugger double. In June 2017, he achieved the rare feat of hitting for the cycle—getting a single, double, triple, and a home run in the same game. He also batted in 125 runs for the third season in a row—the first Rockies player, and the first ever third baseman, to do so. The 2018 season started well. *Sports Illustrated* ranked him the eighth top player and he earned another selection to the MLB All-Star Game, his fourth overall.

COLLECTING HONORS

A fractured finger meant that Arenado played only 111 games of the 2014 season, but he still found time to add another Gold Glove to his haul. Arenado showed his stuff at the beginning of the 2015 season with an incredible catch against the San Francisco Giants that earned him a standing ovation. It was also the season when he put himself among the league leaders for homers and slugging. Ending 2015 tied with Bryce Harper at 42 homers and leading the National League in RBIs, he picked up a Gold Glove and a Silver Slugger.

Arenado in action against the Philadelphia Phillies at Citizens Bank Park in June 2018.

▶▶▶▶▶ FAST FACT ▶▶▶▶▶

Arenado has a Cuban background, but opted to play for the USA in the 2017 World Baseball Classic where he picked up a gold medal.

GIANCARLO STANTON

IF IT'S big hitters you want, then look no further than Stanton. This **SLUGGER** has a reputation for **IMMENSE PHYSICAL STRENGTH** and an ability to **HIT FOR POWER,** many of them out of the park.

NEW YORK YANKEES

LEFT/RIGHT FIELDER

D.O.B: NOVEMBER 8, 1989

MLB DEBUT: JUNE 8, 2010

HEIGHT: 6'6"

WEIGHT: 245 LBS

THROWS: RIGHT

BATS: RIGHT

STANTON 27

STAT ATTACK

	AB	R	H	HR	RBI	SB	AVG	OBP	OPS
2018 (REGULAR SEASON)	617	102	164	38	100	5	.266	.343	.852
MLB CAREER	4,194	678	1,124	305	772	41	.268	.358	.905

MINOR LEAGUE IMPACT

In 2007, Stanton chose not to go to college after the Florida Marlins picked him as part of the amateur draft. He spent the next three seasons playing for various minor league teams around Florida, earning a reputation as a hard hitting slugger. In one game in May 2010, he smashed a home run against the Montgomery Biscuits that cleared the scoreboard and traveled an incredible 550 feet. His performances in the minor leagues soon brought him to the attention of the media who branded him not only the number one prospect in the Marlins' system, but also across the country as a whole. Little wonder that the Marlins soon called him up for his major league debut.

MARLINS TO YANKEES

Stanton finished the 2017 season with 59 home runs, 132 RBIs, a batting average of .281, and winning the National League's MVP award. Despite a stellar 2017 season, a change in the Marlins' ownership led to Stanton being traded to the Yankees, becoming only the second player to be traded after hitting 50 or more home runs in a season (Greg Vaughn being the first). But that didn't hold him back and at the start of the 2018 season, he hit two home runs in his first game for the Yankees, including one in his very first at-bat. In May 2018, he recorded his 1,000th hit.

Stanton dives to catch the ball during a game against the Los Angeles Angels at Yankee Stadium, New York, in May 2018.

>>>>> FAST FACT >>>>>

In 2014, *Stanton made sporting history when he signed the richest contract in team sports history. Spread over 13 years, it was worth an enormous $325 million.*

HOME RUN HERO

Stanton's very first home run was a grand slam against the Tampa Bay Rays, and in doing so he became only the fourth player in the past 25 years to score a home run before the age of 21. In 2012, Stanton was selected for the MLB All-Star Game, the first of four All-Star appearances. His time with the Marlins saw Stanton collect a host of records and awards, including two Silver Slugger Awards and two NL Hank Aaron Awards.

J.D. MARTINEZ

With a reputation as one of the best **POWER HITTERS** in the sport, Martinez is moving to Boston in the hope that he can raise the Red Sox **UP TO CHALLENGE** the Yankees in the AL East. And coming off a season where he posted **45 HOME RUNS** in just 119 games, there aren't many people betting against him!

BOSTON RED SOX

OUTFIELDER/DESIGNATED HITTER

D.O.B: AUGUST 21, 1987

MLB DEBUT: JULY 30, 2011

HEIGHT: 6'3"

WEIGHT: 220 LBS

THROWS: RIGHT

BATS: RIGHT

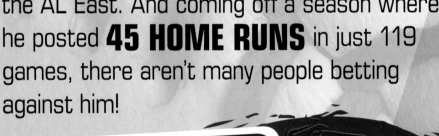

J.D. MARTINEZ 28

STAT ATTACK

	AB	R	H	HR	RBI	SB	AVG	OBP	OPS
2018 (REGULAR SEASON)	569	111	188	43	130	6	.330	.402	1.031
MLB CAREER	3,397	502	993	195	606	22	.292	.353	.886

UPS AND DOWNS

In 2009, Martinez was signed by the Houston Astros as part of the MLB amateur draft. He spent two seasons in the minor league, before his performances earned him promotion to the majors in July 2011. And he made an immediate impression, driving in 20 RBIs in August and setting a new Astros rookie record for one month. Despite this promising start, things tailed off for Martinez and he was released by the team on March 22, 2014. Two days after being released by the Astros, Martinez was signed by the Detroit Tigers on a minor league contract. In less than a month, his performances earned him a call-up to the majors, going on to finish the 2014 season with a .315 batting average, 23 home runs, and 76 RBIs.

RED-SOX ROSTER

In July 2017, Martinez was traded to the Arizona Diamondbacks, where he continued his hard-hitting home run ways. In September that year, he hit his 40th home run of the season, becoming only the fifth player to score 40 or more home runs while playing for two different teams in a single season. After the end of the 2017 season, Martinez became a free agent, and the Red Sox snapped him up in February 2018 with a five-year $110 million contract. His performances in the first part of the 2018 season earned selection to the MLB All-Star Game.

⟫⟫⟫⟫ FAST FACT ⟫⟫⟫⟫

On September 14, 2017, Martinez became only the 18th man in MLB history to hit four home runs in a single game, against the Los Angeles Dodgers.

Martinez hits a home run against the Houston Astros in June 2018.

STRENGTH TO STRENGTH

Martinez had a stellar 2015. He won the Silver Slugger Award, scored 38 home runs (the third highest for a Tigers outfielder), and had 102 RBIs (more than any other Tigers outfielder). He was also a finalist for that season's Gold Glove Award, but lost out to Kole Calhoun of the Angels. Injury limited his appearances in the 2016 season to just 120 games, but he still managed to hit .307 with 22 home runs and 68 RBIs.

PAUL GOLDSCHMIDT

Considered by many as the best all-around first baseman, **"GOLDY"** is a modest player with a habit of grabbing glory. He's a six-time **ALL-STAR,** three-time **GOLD GLOVE** and Silver Slugger award-winner, and he's twice been runner-up for the NL **MOST VALUABLE PLAYER.**

ARIZONA DIAMONDBACKS

FIRST BASEMAN

D.O.B: SEPTEMBER 10, 1987

MLB DEBUT: AUGUST 1, 2011

HEIGHT: 6'3"

WEIGHT: 225 LBS

THROWS: RIGHT

BATS: RIGHT

GOLDSCHMIDT
44

STAT ATTACK

	AB	R	H	HR	RBI	SB	AVG	OBP	OPS
2018 (REGULAR SEASON)	593	95	172	33	83	7	.290	.389	.922
MLB CAREER	3,975	709	1,182	209	710	124	.297	.398	.930

FROM BOBCATS TO MINORS

Born in Delaware but brought up in Texas, Goldschmidt had a very impressive college baseball career. Playing for the Texas State Bobcats in the Southland Conference, he was named league hitter of the year in 2008 and 2009. The Diamondbacks picked him in the eighth round of the 2009 MLB Amateur draft and placed him with the Missoula Osprey of the Rookie League. He had an excellent half-season there, hitting .334 and 18 home runs, along with 62 RBIs. Goldy's form in the minors continued in 2010 with Visalia Rawhide of the California League. He hit .314 with 35 home runs and 108 RBIs, ending the season as the league's MVP, a Minor-League All-Star, and the Diamondbacks' Minor League Player of the Year.

GOLD AND SILVER

He was among the best in the league in 2013 for RBIs and was rewarded with his first All-Star selection, a Gold Glove, and a Silver Slugger. Goldy returned from injury in 2015 to record his 100th career home run and repeat his Gold Glove and Silver Slugger success. His star has continued to rise in the past two seasons and, in August 2017, he put in a superb performance, hitting three home runs for the first time against the Chicago Cubs. The year 2018 started slowly, but soon picked up as Goldschmidt was selected to start for the NL All-Star Team for a sixth consecutive year.

>>>>> FAST FACT >>>>>

In September 2013, *Goldschmidt graduated from university with a Bachelor of Science degree in management.*

BIG-MONEY DEALS

Following his standout minors performance, Goldschmidt made his debut with Arizona on August 1, 2011 against the San Francisco Giants. Goldschmidt singled in his first at-bat, and finished the season having batted .250 with eight home runs and 26 RBIs in 48 games. In 2012, Goldschmidt batted an impressive .286 with 20 home runs, 82 runs, 82 RBIs, 43 doubles, and 18 stolen bases. That led the Diamondbacks to sign him for another five years in a $32-million deal.

Goldschmidt watches his single fly in the third inning against the Colorado Rockies in July 2018.

MOOKIE BETTS

They say size isn't **EVERYTHING**, and Marcus Lynn "Mookie" Betts may just prove them right. He may not be the biggest guy, but what he lacks in **SIZE** he more than makes up for with **SPEED**, energy, and **ENTHUSIASM**. Combine those with one of the most powerful and **FASTEST SWINGS** in the league, and you have one of the best all-around players in the league today.

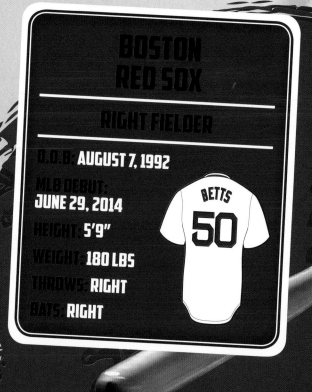

BOSTON RED SOX

RIGHT FIELDER

D.O.B: AUGUST 7, 1992

MLB DEBUT: JUNE 29, 2014

HEIGHT: 5'9"

WEIGHT: 180 LBS

THROWS: RIGHT

BATS: RIGHT

BETTS 50

STAT ATTACK

	AB	R	H	HR	RBI	SB	AVG	OBP	OPS
2018 (REGULAR SEASON)	520	129	180	32	80	30	.346	.438	1.078
MLB CAREER	2,606	478	789	110	390	110	.303	.370	.888

SPORTS MAD

When it comes to sports, Betts tried (and excelled) in more before the age of 25 than most people manage in a lifetime. Growing up, he was always playing with a ball of some sort. At school, basketball was his true love, but he also played football. And then there's golf, and table tennis, and pool, and bowling. However, Betts has been fully focused on baseball since making his MLB debut in June 2014.

ALL-STAR STREAK

Betts continued 2017 in top form with a streak of 129 plate appearances without a strikeout that stretched back to September 2016. This was the longest run in MLB since 2004. It finally ended in the fourth inning of a 3-0 loss against the Toronto Blue Jays. He finished the season with a .264 batting average and recorded 101 runs, 26 stolen bases, 24 home runs, and 102 RBIs. In 2018, he set a Red Sox record for three-homer games, when he recorded his fourth against the Royals, and became the first MLB player in history to do so before the age of 26.

SEEING RED

In his first full season in MLB he hit .291 with five home runs—the first of which came on July 2 against the Chicago Cubs. The following month he hit his first grand slam, against the Tampa Bay Rays, making him the youngest Red Sox player to hit a grand slam in 49 years. The following season, he hit a home run in the opener against the Philadelphia Phillies and ended the season with a .291 batting average, with 92 runs scored, 77 runs batted in, 18 home runs, and 21 stolen bases. By 2016, Betts was really getting into his stride, becoming an All-Star for the first time, and was runner-up in the AL Player of the Year awards, coming second to Mike Trout.

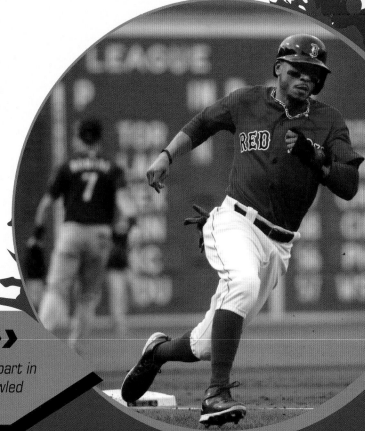

Betts rounds third, storming past Seattle Mariners third baseman Kyle Seager in June 2018.

>>>>> FAST FACT >>>>>

Betts is a keen and talented bowler and has taken part in the PBA World Series of Bowling twice. He's also bowled three perfect games, scoring 300.

JOEY VOTTO

During **12 SEASONS** in MLB, Votto has collected enough **HARDWARE** to fill a trophy cabinet. He's a **SIX-TIME MLB ALL-STAR,** a seven-time Tip O'Neill Award winner, and he collected the **NL MVP AWARD** in 2010. He's also recognized as one of the best hitters in action in the league.

CINCINNATI REDS

FIRST BASEMAN

D.O.B: SEPTEMBER 10, 1983

MLB DEBUT: SEPTEMBER 4, 2007

HEIGHT: 6'2"

WEIGHT: 220 LBS

THROWS: RIGHT

BATS: LEFT

VOTTO
19

STAT ATTACK

	AB	R	H	HR	RBI	SB	AVG	OBP	OPS
2018 (REGULAR SEASON)	503	67	143	12	67	2	.284	.417	.837
MLB CAREER	5,563	930	1,729	269	897	74	.311	.427	.957

STRONG STARTER

A native of Toronto, Canada, Votto played high school baseball at Richview Collegiate Institute, where he also excelled at basketball and hockey. In 2002, he was selected straight out of high school in the amateur draft by the Cincinnati Reds. After five seasons in the minor leagues, he was called up by the Reds to make his debut in September 2007 against the Mets and went on to finish that year batting .321 for 4 home runs and 17 RBIs. His rookie season in 2008 saw him settle in and soar, finishing second in the National League Rookie of the Year voting and breaking the Reds record for the most runs batted in by a rookie in a season.

RECORD SETTER

Over the next 12 seasons with the Reds, Votto has racked up record after record. The only low was the 2014 season, when injury limited Votto to just 62 games when he batted a career-low of .255 with just 6 home runs and 23 RBIs. Other than that, he has consistently posted great numbers, leading the National League in on-base percentages in no fewer than six seasons, and in walks in five seasons.

HOME HITTER

During his career with the Reds, Votto has built a reputation as a clutch hitter, scoring decisive runs when it really matters. Showing great patience at the plate, he knows when to hit the ball and where to hit it, lashing out at the very last moment to connect before the ball can hit the catcher's glove. No wonder he's won the Hank Aaron Award for the league's best hitter. In the field, he's recognized as a superb and agile defensive first baseman and has led the league in assists for that position in three seasons (2008, 2011, and 2012).

Votto fields a single in the first inning, playing Chicago Cubs, in Cincinnati in June 2018.

⟩⟩⟩⟩⟩ FAST FACT ⟩⟩⟩⟩⟩

In 2012, Votto signed a 10-year, $225 million extension, which, at the time, was the longest active deal in baseball and made Votto the highest paid athlete from Canada.

PITCHING ACES

These guys know what it takes to **DOMINATE A GAME.** And they'll use a whole arsenal of **DIFFERENT PITCHES** whether it be a curve ball, fast ball, slider, or **KNUCKLEBALL** so that they know exactly what pitch to **THROW TO WHICH BATTER** with devastating effect.

CLAYTON KERSHAW

LOS ANGELES DODGERS

POSITION: STARTING PITCHER
EARNED RUN AVERAGE: 2.39

One of the finest pitchers of the modern era, the Los Angeles Dodgers' Clayton Kershaw is a three-time winner of the Cy Young Award, and was the NL's Most Valuable Player in 2014. A methodical perfectionist, his deliveries are lethal, deceptive, and vary in speed. This seven-time All-Star has an incredible lifetime ERA of 2.39, which is the lowest of any starting pitcher in MLB since 1920.

MAX SCHERZER

WASHINGTON NATIONALS

POSITION: STARTING PITCHER
EARNED RUN AVERAGE: 3.22

Nationals starting pitcher Scherzer is at the top of his game. Equipped with four pitching styles, the former Arizona Diamondbacks and Detroit Tigers player is a six-time All-Star. He is also the winner of two Cy Young Awards (2013 and 2016), and is a three-time Wins Leader (2013, 2014, and 2016).

CHRIS SALE

BOSTON RED SOX

POSITION: STARTING PITCHER
EARNED RUN AVERAGE: 2.89

Red Sox starting pitcher Chris Sale is a seven-time All-Star (2012–2018) and led the American League in strikeouts in 2015 and 2017. Nicknamed "The Condor," Sale made headlines when he became the first pitcher in the American League to rack up 300 strikeouts in a season since 1999.

JACOB DEGROM

NEW YORK METS

POSITION: STARTING PITCHER
EARNED RUN AVERAGE: 2.67

Having been named NL Rookie of the Year for 2014, Jacob deGrom hasn't held back in his performances since then. A career ERA of 2.67 and almost 1,000 strikeouts saw him selected to the 2015 All-Star Game. And even cutting off his famous long hair after the 2017 season hasn't held him back as he led the MLB with an ERA of 1.68 at the start of the 2018 season, earning another All-Star call-up.

JUSTIN VERLANDER

HOUSTON ASTROS

POSITION: STARTING PITCHER
EARNED RUN AVERAGE: 3.39

A seven-time All-Star (2007, 2009–2013, 2018), a World Series champion (2017), an AL MVP (2011), an AL Cy Young Award (2011), and an AL Rookie of the Year (2006)—it's safe to say that Verlander has won pretty much everything you can win as an MLB pitcher. But that doesn't mean he's starting to slow down. In May 2018, he recorded his 2,500th strikeout and selection to another All-Star Game.

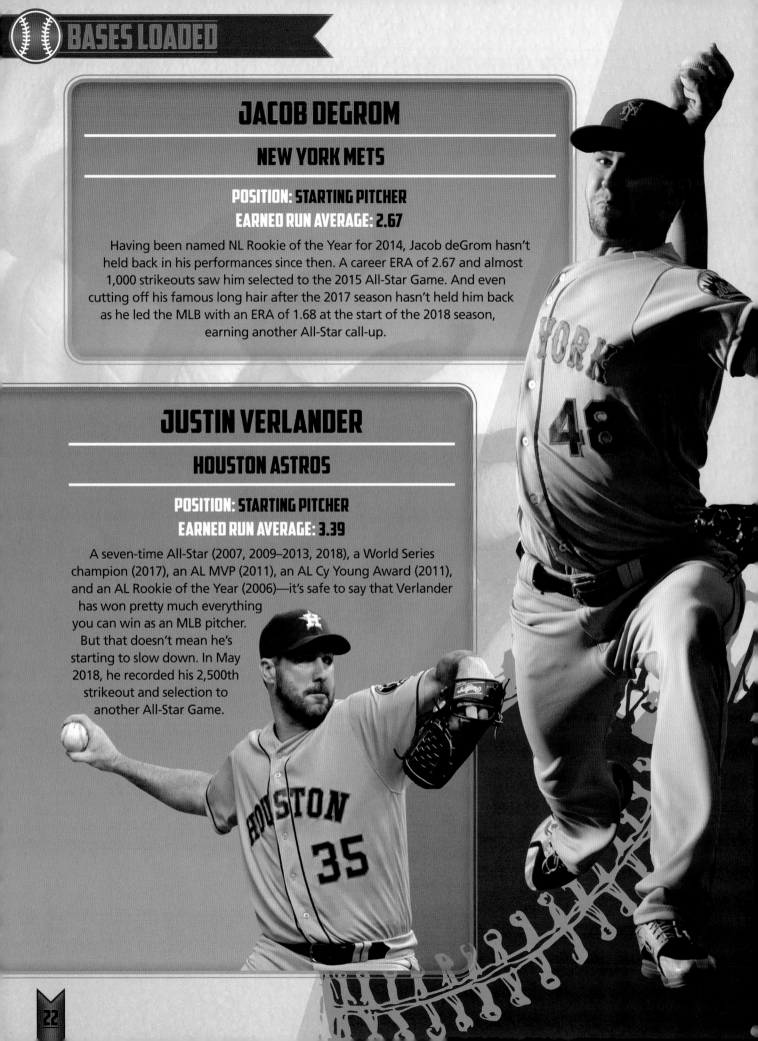

COREY KLUBER

CLEVELAND INDIANS

POSITION: STARTING PITCHER
EARNED RUN AVERAGE: 3.09

Kluber has a tough, no-nonsense personality on the mound that's earned him the nickname "Klubot." He can dominate with any one of his five pitches, and his performances have earned him three All-Star appearances (2016–2018) and a Cy Young Award in both 2014 and 2017. He was the AL Wins Leader in both 2014 and 2017 and an AL ERA leader in 2017.

ALBERT PUJOLS

During **11 SEASONS** with the Cardinals, and seven more with the Angels, José Alberto Pujols Alcántra has **SEEN IT ALL** and won it all—two World Series, **THREE ML MVPS**, and ten All-Star appearances. On top of that he's won six **SILVER SLUGGER** Awards, two Hank Aaron Awards, and been **NL BATTING CHAMPION.** He's got one full trophy cabinet!

LOS ANGELES ANGELS

FIRST BASEMAN

D.O.B: JANUARY 16, 1980

MLB DEBUT: APRIL 2, 2001

HEIGHT: 6'3"

WEIGHT: 240 LBS

THROWS: RIGHT

BATS: RIGHT

PUJOLS 5

STAT ATTACK

	AB	R	H	HR	RBI	SB	AVG	OBP	OPS
2018 (REGULAR SEASON)	465	50	114	19	64	1	.245	.289	.700
MLB CAREER	10,196	1,773	3,082	633	1,982	111	.302	.382	.936

ALL-AROUND ALL-STAR

Moving from the Dominican Republic at the age of 16, Pujols and his family eventually settled in Independence, Missouri. At Fort Osage High School, he batted over .500 in his first season and went on to earn all-state honors twice. After just one season in college, he was selected by the Cardinals in the 13th round of the 1999 MLB Draft. His performances in the minors drew plenty of attention, and legend has it that Cardinals superstar Mark McGwire told manager Tony La Russa that if he didn't promote Pujols "it might be one of the worst moves of your career."

RECORD BREAKER

Throughout his career, Pujols has set record after record after record. His stats rank him in the Top 10 major league players of all time in total bases, home runs, and RBIs. He holds a fielding percentage of .994, as well as a single season major league record of 185 assists, set in 2009. And when it's not the stats that are singing his praises, it's other MLB players and coaches. He's been named the most feared hitter in baseball by MLB managers, while fellow player Joey Votto described him as "one of the greatest hitters of all time."

Pujols celebrates after an incredible two-run home run in a game against the Seattle Mariners in July 2018.

FLYING START

In his rookie season, Pujols posted incredible figures, batting .329 with 194 hits, 47 doubles, 37 home runs, 112 runs, and selection to the All-Star game. And since then he hasn't looked back. In 2003, he played in what was to be the first of eight consecutive All-Star games. Three years after that, he won his first World Series, which he repeated five years later in 2011. After the 2011 season, Pujols became a free agent, and the Angels broke the bank by offering him a 10-year, $254 million contract. In 2018, he passed a number of landmarks, recording his 10,000th career at-bat and his 3,000th major league hit.

▶▶▶▶▶ FAST FACT ▶▶▶▶▶

When batting against right-handed pitchers, Pujols uses a 32.5-ounce bat, but switches to a 33-ounce bat against left-handers to avoid pulling the ball when he swings.

ADRIAN BELTRÉ

In a career spanning **20 SEASONS** in MLB, Beltré has played for teams on the west coast, the east coast, and now in the **LONE STAR STATE.** In that time, he's made four All-Star appearances and won five **GOLD GLOVE AWARDS**, two Platinum Awards, four Silver Slugger Awards, and is a member of the 3,000 hit club.

TEXAS RANGERS

THIRD BASEMAN

APRIL 7, 1979

MLB DEBUT JUNE 24, 1998

5'11"

220 LBS

RIGHT

RIGHT

BELTRÉ
29

STAT ATTACK

	AB	R	H	HR	RBI	SB	AVG	OBP	OPS
2018 (REGULAR SEASON)	433	49	118	15	65	1	.273	.328	.763
MLB CAREER	11,068	1,524	3,166	477	1,707	121	.286	.339	.819

SCOUTING FIND

Beltré was spotted at the age of just 15 while he was attending a Los Angeles Dodgers facility and was signed straight away. Four years later, he became the youngest player in the National League at the time, when he made his debut against the Anaheim Angels. After six consistent seasons with the Dodgers, 2004 proved a breakout season for Beltré. He finished the season leading the league with 48 home runs, and had a batting average of .334, with 200 hits, 121 RBIs, and 103 runs scored. He was runner-up in the voting for the NL MVP and won his first Silver Slugger Award.

MOVING NORTH

The Seattle Mariners signed Beltré as a free agent for the 2005 season. His six seasons at Safeco Field were far from his best, but he still managed to secure a Gold Glove Award, and two Fielding Bible Awards for his defensive performances in the field. On November 5, 2009, he declared himself a free agent again and was signed by the Red Sox on a one-year, $9 million deal. He finished the 2010 season leading the team with a batting average of .321.

Beltré swings for the ball in a 2018 MLB game against the Toronto Blue Jays in Arlington, Texas.

LONE STAR SUPERSTAR

In January 2011, Beltré joined the Texas Rangers. In May 2014, he hit his 100th home run, becoming only the fifth to score 100 home runs with three different teams. In September that year, he overtook Vladimir Guerrero to become the all-time hit leader for Dominican-born players. He went on to collect his 3,000th hit against the Orioles on July 30, 2017. Other accomplishments include being the league's all-time hit leader for a foreign-born player, the fourth third baseman to record 1,500 RBIs, and only the second player to record a three-home-run game and a cycle in the same week.

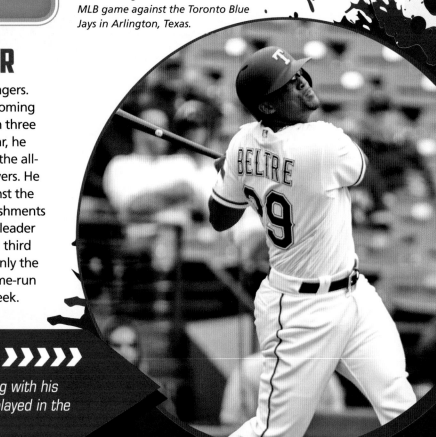

>>>>> FAST FACT >>>>>

Beltré is one of two active players, along with his Ranger teammate Bartolo Colón, to have played in the major leagues in the 1990s.

MIKE TROUT

SOME SAY the Trout is one of the **BEST MLB** players of his generation. Others say he's the best in the entire history of baseball—period! Trout uses a mix of height, **POWER, STRENGTH, AND SPEED** to dominate the plate, becoming a **SEVEN-TIME ALL-STAR** and an **AL MOST-VALUABLE PLAYER.**

LOS ANGELES ANGELS

THIRD BASEMAN

D.O.B: APRIL 16, 1991

MLB DEBUT: APRIL 28, 2013

HEIGHT: 6'2"

WEIGHT: 235 LBS

THROWS: RIGHT

BATS: RIGHT

TROUT
27

STAT ATTACK

	AB	R	H	HR	RBI	SB	AVG	OBP	OPS
2018 (REGULAR SEASON)	471	101	147	39	79	24	.312	.460	1.088
MLB CAREER	3,870	793	1187	240	648	189	.307	.416	.990

SCHOOL THUNDERBOLT

A native of New Jersey, Trout went to Millville Senior High where he played baseball for the school's Thunderbolts sports team. As a pitcher, he tossed a no-hitter against Egg Harbor Township High School and hit 18 home runs—a New Jersey high-school record. Trout was set to go to East Carolina University before being drafted by the Angels in 2009. Trout's rookie season was spectacular, as he set records all over the field. Brought up from the minors in April 2012, he played three four-hit games in June, ending the month as the AL Player and Rookie of the Month.

NUMBER ONE ALL-STAR

He is the first player to pick up the All-Star MVP award in consecutive seasons (2014 and 2015) and only the sixth player in MLB history to win the regular MVP and the All-Star MVP awards in the same season (2014). Just before the start of the 2018 season, *Sports Illustrated* ranked him as the number one player in MLB, and he's still not slowing down. He had his first five-hit game against the Yankees on May 26, then in two games against Seattle in June, he homered twice in consecutive games for the first time in his career. Needless to say, he was called up for the 2018 MLB All-Star Game for the seventh consecutive year.

>>>>> FAST FACT >>>>>

Trout enjoys hunting and fishing, and he's a big fan of sharing weather stats and tracking storms. He's also an avid football fan and is an Eagles season ticket holder.

Trout has homered in four of the six games he has played on his birthday—in 2012, 2013, 2015, and 2017.

GREATEST ROOKIE?

At age 21, he became the first player in MLB history to hit 30 home runs, steal 45 bases, and score 125 runs in one season. He was voted AL Rookie of the Year, making him the youngest-ever winner of the award. Since then, he's been an All-Star player in every full season of his MLB career, and has joined the likes of Ted Williams, Mickey Mantle, and Joe DiMaggio in making three All-Star appearances before the age of 24.

WORLD SERIES STARS

It takes a **SPECIAL KIND** of player to **STEP UP TO THE PLATE** when you're at the business end of the season. The World Series pits the **TWO BEST TEAMS** in the league against each other and these players have shown that they've got what it takes to be the **BEST OF THE BEST** and be triumphant in winning the World Series.

ANTHONY RIZZO

CHICAGO CUBS

POSITION: FIRST BASEMAN
BATTING AVERAGE: .270

Chicago Cubs first baseman Rizzo was drafted by the Boston Red Sox back in 2007. But it's only since his move to the Cubs in 2012 that his full potential has been realized. Now a three-time All-Star and 2016 World Series champion, Rizzo is up there with the best in his position. In July 2018, he even gave pitching a try, and managed to retire A.J. Pollock of the Diamondbacks!

JOSE ALTUVE

HOUSTON ASTROS

POSITION: SECOND BASEMAN | BATTING AVERAGE: .316

Altuve makes up for what he lacks in height with superb defending skills and awesome power at bat. A five-time All-Star, he has been the AL's batting champion three times and the stolen base leader twice. He has won three Silver Slugger Awards, and picked up the Gold Glove for his position in 2015.

MADISON BUMGARNER

SAN FRANCISCO GIANTS

POSITION: STARTING PITCHER

PITCHING AVERAGE: 3.03

"MadBum" is a giant in every sense. A three-time World Series winner, he is also a four-time All-Star and winner of the Silver Slugger twice. His World Series performances are particularly special, going 4-0 and striking out 31, giving him an incredible World Series ERA of .250.

GLEYBER TORRES

After moving from his **HOME COUNTRY** of Venezuela, Gleyber Torres has **BLAZED A PATH** first through the minors and now into MLB itself. He's already been made an **ALL-STAR** in his very first season and his performances **ON THE FIELD** promise a lot more to come.

NEW YORK YANKEES

SECOND BASEMAN/SHORTSTOP

D.O.B: DECEMBER 13, 1996

MLB DEBUT: APRIL 22, 2018

HEIGHT: 6'1"

WEIGHT: 200 LBS

THROWS: RIGHT

BATS: RIGHT

TORRES
25

STAT ATTACK

	AB	R	H	HR	RBI	SB	AVG	OBP	OPS
2018 (REGULAR SEASON)	431	54	117	24	77	6	.271	.340	.820
MLB CAREER	431	54	117	24	77	6	.271	.340	.820

EARLY STARTER

Growing up in Caracas, Venezuela, Torres earned his unique first name because his father, Eusebio, was fascinated by the name "Qleyber." He started playing baseball from an early age, taking the field at the age of four as a center fielder, catcher, pitcher, and shortstop. In high school, he showed a talent for basketball, but his father persuaded him to drop that in favor of baseball. Moving up to the Caribbean coast and the city of Maracay, Torres attended an academy that had links with many MLB scouts. And it was here that he came to the attention of the Chicago Cubs who offered him a contract.

TO THE MAJORS

The 2017 season came to an early end in June, when Torres tore an elbow ligament while trying to slide headfirst into home. The injury needed surgery that ruled him out for the rest of the season. The next season got off to a much better start, when the Yankees called him up to the majors to face the Blue Jays in his debut. He needed less than two weeks to hit his first home run, and on May 25, he hit a home run in his fourth straight game, becoming the youngest player in American League history to do so. His rookie performance earned him a call-up to the 2018 All-Star Game.

Torres throws to first base and records an out in the first inning against the Texas Rangers, in May 2018.

MINORS STAR

Signing Torres as an international free agent for a $1.7 million signing bonus, the Cubs sent their new talent out to the minors, where he played for a string of teams, all the time working his way up the leagues. By the time he was 19 years old, he had been traded to the Yankees and was the youngest player in the Arizona Fall League (AFL) and became the youngest to win the AFL MVP Award in 2016.

>>>>> FAST FACT >>>>>

As a child, one of Torres' favorite games was "chapitas," which involves one person pitching a bottle cap which another would try to hit with a broomstick.

SHOHEI OHTANI

This is one player who has **ALL THE SKILLS** to become a baseball great—**A STRONG ARM** from the outfield and a devastating **POWERFUL BATTING STYLE** to smash anything out of the field. But get him **ON THE MOUND** and watch his pitches **BLAST THROUGH** any of the opposing teams' batting lineup.

LOS ANGELES ANGELS

PITCHER/DESIGNATED HITTER/OUTFIELDER

D.O.B: JULY 5, 1994

MLB DEBUT: MARCH 29, 2018

HEIGHT: 6'4"

WEIGHT: 200 LBS

THROWS: RIGHT

BATS: LEFT

OHTANI 17

STAT ATTACK

	W	L	ERA	G	GS	SV	IP	SO	WHIP
2018 (REGULAR SEASON)	4	2	3.31	10	10	0	51.2	.63	1.16
MLB CAREER	4	2	3.31	10	10	0	51.2	63	1.16

POWER PITCHER

Even in high school in his native Japan, Ohtani showed that he had something of a golden arm, setting a new record for the fastest pitch by a Japanese high school pitcher with a blistering speed of 99 mph. Even at this early age, he drew the attention of several MLB teams, including the Texas Rangers, Boston Red Sox, Los Angeles Dodgers, and the New York Yankees. However, the Hokkaido Nippo-Ham Fighters of Nippon Professional Baseball's (NPB) Pacific League were also determined to sign the pitching star and, after a long negotiation, Ohtani signed for the Fighters for the 2013 season.

BIG-HITTER

By 2017, Ohtani was pushing for a move to the MLB and in December that year he signed for the Los Angeles Angels, starting on Opening Day as the designated hitter against the Oakland Athletics. He singled in his first at-bat and, within a week, he had become the first Angels player to homer in his first two home career games. On April 1, he made his pitching debut, striking out six batters on his way to his first MLB win. In his second start on the mound a week later, he recorded a perfect game for more than six innings before allowing a hit.

ALL-AROUND MASTER

As a recognized pitcher, position player, and batter, Ohtani set several records all over the field. He was only the second rookie to be used as both a pitcher and as a position player, and the first NPB player since 1963 to pitch and bat third, fourth, or fifth. His strong arm saw him used as an outfielder regularly and his pitches become faster and faster. The 2016 season proved a breakout year for Ohtani as a batter. He recorded 22 home runs, 67 RBIs, 65 runs, and had seven stolen bases.

Ohtani bunts foul in the second inning, playing against the Los Angeles Dodgers in July 2018.

⟫⟫⟫ FAST FACT ⟫⟫⟫

Ohtani holds the record for the fastest pitch for a Japanese pitcher, recording 102.5 mph while playing in the NPB.

VLADIMIR GUERRERO JR.

He's yet to **SWING A BAT** in the majors, but **HIS HERITAGE** and the numbers he's putting together in the minors mean that Vladimir Guerrero Jr. is definitely one player you'll want to **KEEP YOUR EYES ON.** It's only a matter of time before he takes the **STEP UP** to the big leagues.

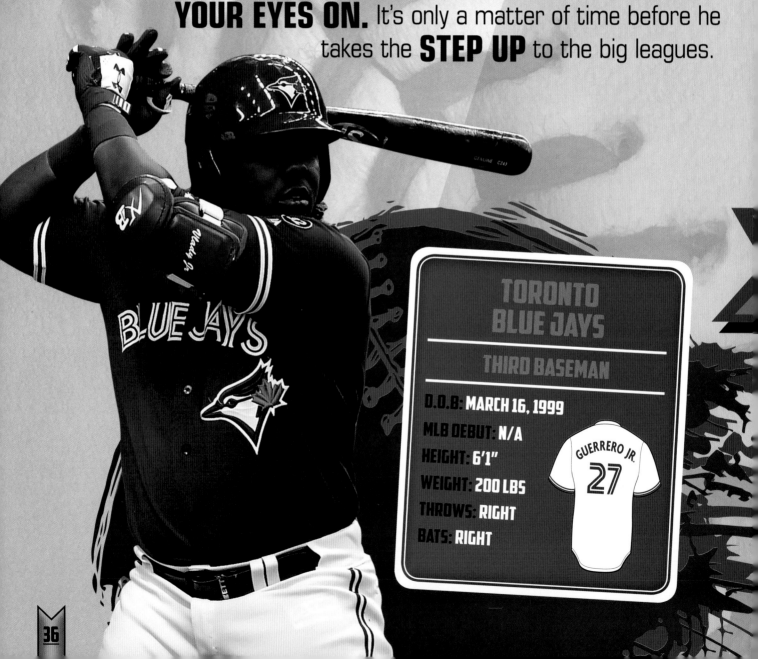

TORONTO BLUE JAYS

THIRD BASEMAN

D.O.B: MARCH 16, 1999

MLB DEBUT: N/A

HEIGHT: 6'1"

WEIGHT: 200 LBS

THROWS: RIGHT

BATS: RIGHT

GUERRERO JR. 27

STAT ATTACK

	AB	R	H	HR	RBI	SB	AVG	OBP	OPS
2018 (REGULAR SEASON)	357	67	136	20	78	3	.381	.437	1.073
MiLB CAREER	1,030	183	341	41	200	26	.331	.414	.943

POWERFUL PEDIGREE

Vladimir Guerrero Jr. is following in some pretty big footsteps as he works his way up to the majors. His father is none other than Vladimir Guerrero, who spent 16 seasons in MLB for the Expos, Angels, Rangers, and Orioles. This nine-time All-Star was also voted American League MVP in 2004 and, in a poll of 30 major league managers in 2008, he was voted one of the most feared hitters in baseball. No wonder that Guerrero Sr. was inducted into the National Baseball Hall of Fame in 2018. And if that wasn't enough Guerrero Jr. is also the nephew of MLB star Wilton Guerrero and the cousin of Gabriel Guerrero, a prospect with the Cincinnati Reds.

UP THROUGH THE LEAGUES

The 2017 season saw Guerrero Jr. rise up through the minor leagues, first with the Class-A Lansing Lugnuts, then to the Advanced-A Dunedin Blue Jays, then with the Double-A New Hampshire Fisher Cats, before it was announced that he was moving up to the Triple-A Buffalo Bisons. In that time, he has consistently posted great figures. In 61 games with New Hampshire, he hit .402 with 14 home runs, and 60 RBIs. So it's hardly surprising that he has been branded a top prospect by MLB, ESPN, and *Baseball America*. Watch out for this guy!

Guerrero Jr. celebrates a home run during the ninth inning of a game against the St. Louis Cardinals in March 2018.

>>>>> FAST FACT >>>>>

Guerrero Jr. had only just turned 16 when he was signed by the Toronto Blue Jays on July 2, 2015 for a signing bonus of $3.9 million.

MINOR STARTER

Making his minors debut on June 23, 2016 for the Rookie Advanced Bluefield Blue Jays, Guerrero Jr. hit his first home run the following day against the Bristol Pirates. On August 12, he recorded his first multi-homer game, hitting two against the Pulanski Pirates. Through the 2016 season, he played 62 games, posting an average of .271, with eight home runs, 46 RBIs, and 15 stolen bases.

ONES TO WATCH

They may not **GRAB ALL THE HEADLINES,** but these guys know how to make **AN IMPACT** on the field. They've quietly gone about **THEIR BUSINESS** making plays when it matters most, showing that they're prepared to give it **ALL THEY'VE GOT** for their team.

MANNY MACHADO

LOS ANGELES DODGERS

POSITION: THIRD BASEMAN/SHORTSTOP

BATTING AVERAGE: .282

A standout defensive player, Machado has made his name as a top third baseman and shortstop in MLB. Since his debut in 2012, he's picked up two AL Gold Glove Awards, the Platinum Glove in 2013, and four All-Star appearances. In July 2018, he moved west and joined the Dodgers, changing his number from 13 to 8 because he's a huge Kobe Bryant fan.

BRYCE HARPER

WASHINGTON NATIONALS

POSITION: RIGHT FIELDER

BATTING AVERAGE:
.279

Since debuting in 2012, the six-time All-Star right fielder for the Nationals has come through as one of the best "five-toolers" in MLB. Known for hammering homers, he picked up the 2012 Rookie of the Year award and was the youngest right fielder picked for the All-Stars.

CHARLIE BLACKMON

COLORADO ROCKIES

POSITION: CENTER FIELDER

BATTING AVERAGE:
.302

The three-time All-Star and two-time Silver Slugger Award winner knows how to hit. In September 2017, he homered against the Dodgers, reaching 102 RBI and setting a new major league record for RBIs by a leadoff hitter in one season. Little wonder the Rockies have signed him to a six-year, $108 million contract!

FRANCISCO LINDOR

Three times an **ALL-STAR PICK,** a Gold Glove and **PLATINUM GLOVE** in his second season, a Silver Slugger Award, and an appearance for his home country at the **WORLD BASEBALL CLASSIC—** what more can you say about the man with one of the **BIGGEST SMILES** in world baseball?

CLEVELAND INDIANS

SHORTSTOP

D.O.B: NOVEMBER 14, 1993

MLB DEBUT: JUNE 14, 2015

HEIGHT: 5'11"

WEIGHT: 190 LBS

THROWS: RIGHT

BATS: SWITCH

LINDOR
12

STAT ATTACK

	AB	R	H	HR	RBI	SB	AVG	OBP	OPS
2018 (REGULAR SEASON)	661	129	183	38	92	25	.277	.352	.871
MLB CAREER	2,306	377	665	98	310	71	.288	.350	.837

TOP PROSPECT

Lindor's family moved him from Puerto Rico to the USA when he was 12, hoping to land him a career in baseball. The Cleveland Indians picked him in the 2011 amateur draft while he was still in his senior year of high school and he was signed for $2.9 million. Lindor's time in the minors included an All-Star Futures appearance in 2012 and he was named as the Indians' top prospect in 2013. He made his MLB debut on June 14, 2015, and went on to finish that season as runner-up in the AL Rookie of the Year voting.

WINNING STREAK

The 2017 season brought Lindor another All-Star appearance and, in July, against the Toronto Blue Jays, he hit the first walk-off homer of his career. He went on to hit 30 homers by September 12, helping the Indians to a 20-game winning streak. And 2018 started in much the same way. He had a superb month of May, and his performances earned him AL Player of the Month, leading all players with 44 hits and 27 runs scored. On June 1, against Minnesota, he recorded a second consecutive game where he homered twice and doubled twice, becoming only the fourth major leaguer to do so in MLB history.

Lindor plays second base in a game against the Minnesota Twins in Minneapolis, June 2018.

>>>>> FAST FACT >>>>>

While he generally goes by the nickname "Paquito," Lindor is also sometimes called "Mr. Smile" because of his near-permanent grin!

SUPER SEASON

In 2016, Lindor hit .301 with 15 home runs and 78 RBIs in 158 games—playing a significant part in helping the Indians to their division title. He helped his team sweep aside the Red Sox in the Division Series, going three for 12 with a home run. Lindor's 2016 MLB postseason record was impressive—his seven multi-hit games were the most ever for a player under 23, and he's the youngest Cleveland batter to have six hits in the World Series. With an All-Star call-up, a Gold Glove award, and a World Series appearance, 2016 proved to be a breakthrough season.

CARLOS CORREA

From the **PLAYING FIELDS** of Puerto Rico to the heights of a World Series title, Carlos Correa has used his **POWER, SPEED, AND STAMINA** to post home run after home run on both the **MLB STAGE** and in the international arena.

HOUSTON ASTROS

SHORTSTOP

D.O.B: SEPTEMBER 22, 1994

MLB DEBUT: JUNE 8, 2015

HEIGHT: 6'4"

WEIGHT: 215 LBS

THROWS: RIGHT

BATS: RIGHT

CORREA
1

STAT ATTACK

	AB	R	H	HR	RBI	SB	AVG	OBP	OPS
2018 (REGULAR SEASON)	402	60	96	15	65	3	.239	.323	.728
MLB CAREER	1,788	270	495	81	313	32	.277	.356	.833

MAJOR IMPRESSION

With his family working multiple jobs to support the rising star of Puerto Rico baseball, Correa quickly rose through the ranks of local teams based all over the island. Attention-grabbing performances at the 2011 PG World and National Showcases and the PG WBAA World Championships meant that, despite signing a letter of intent with the University of Miami, he entered the 2012 MLB Draft confident that someone would pick him up. Both ESPN and *Sports Illustrated* made him a top-ten pick and, sure enough, the Astros pounced on Correa, making him the first overall pick and offering him a $4.8 million signing bonus.

TITLE-WINNER

The next season started in style as Correa became the youngest player in Astros' history to hit a home run on Opening Day. He finished the 2016 season with a .274 batting average with 20 home runs and 96 RBIs. He also recorded four walk-off home runs, more than anyone else in MLB. And things got even better in 2017, as Correa helped to guide the Astros to only their second ever World Series. The series against the Dodgers went to the wire, with the Astros clinching Game 7 to record their first World Series win in franchise history.

SERIOUS SLUGGER

During the 2013 and 2014 seasons, Correa worked his way up the minor leagues from the Gulf Coast Astros of the Rookie-level Gulf Coast League up to the Fresno Grizzlies of the Triple A Pacific Coast League. During his time with the Grizzlies, he played 24 games, during which he hit .276 with three home runs and 12 RBIs. On June 8, 2015, the Astros promoted Correa to the big show and a debut against the White Sox, when he managed to record an RBI single. The very next day he stole his first career base and hit his first MLB home run.

Correa keeps his focus during the first inning against the Arizona Diamondbacks in Phoenix, May 2018.

⟩⟩⟩⟩⟩ FAST FACT ⟩⟩⟩⟩⟩

While at the Puerto Rico Baseball Academy, the coaches were so impressed with Correa's skill that they offered the student lifts to school after the family car had been totaled.

JOSÉ RAMÍREZ

Hailing from the Dominican Republic, this **POWER HITTER** was once thought **TOO SMALL** to be a star. He may not be the biggest and he may not have had the **EASIEST RIDE** in Major League Baseball, but his **STYLE AND STATS** have made him a player who is hard to ignore.

CLEVELAND INDIANS

THIRD BASEMAN

D.O.B: SEPTEMBER 17, 1992

MLB DEBUT: SEPTEMBER 1, 2013

HEIGHT: 5'9"

WEIGHT: 165 LBS

THROWS: RIGHT

BATS: SWITCH

RAMÍREZ
11

STAT ATTACK

	AB	R	H	HR	RBI	SB	AVG	OBP	OPS
2018 (REGULAR SEASON)	578	110	156	39	105	34	.270	.387	.939
MLB CAREER	2,292	383	653	87	308	93	.285	.357	.844

DOMINICAN DYNAMITE

Growing up in the Dominican Republic, Ramírez played baseball as a kid in the Dominican Prospect League. A trip to the Cleveland Indians' facility in Boca Chica proved fruitful as he was spotted by a scout and signed by the Indians with a $50,000 signing bonus. After sitting out the 2010 season, he started the 2011 season in the minors with the Arizona Indians, posting .325 in 48 games. Rising rapidly up the minor leagues in 2012, it wasn't long before the Indians called him up to the majors.

STANDOUT YEAR

At the start of the 2017 season, Ramírez signed a five-year contract extension with the Indians worth $26 million. In June, he recorded nine consecutive multi-hit games, the longest streak for an Indians player since 1938, earning him his first call-up to that year's MLB All-Star Game. He helped the Indians record a winning streak of 22 consecutive games, the second longest in MLB history. He finished that year with a .318 batting average, 29 home runs, 83 RBIs, and 107 runs. And he didn't slow down in 2018, earning another selection to the MLB All-Star Game.

UP AND DOWN AND UP

Called up late in the 2013 season, Ramírez helped the Indians grab a wildcard slot and their first playoff berth since 2007. However, he was sent back down to the minors at the start of the 2014 season and spent much of that season and the next moving between the minors and the MLB as the Indians struggled with injuries and form. A late surge toward the end of 2015 was carried into the 2016 season, which proved to be his breakout year. Batting at almost every spot in the Indians' lineup, he helped to steer the team to the World Series against the Cubs, where they lost in Game 7.

Ramírez throws out Pittsburgh Pirates' David Freese at first base during a game in Cleveland in July 2018.

>>>>> FAST FACT >>>>>

Of the 74 MLB hitters who posted at least 25 home runs during the 2017 season, Ramírez struck out the fewest times, with only 69.

HOW WELL DO YOU KNOW THE MLB?

Test your knowledge of the MLB's star players and teams and see just how much you know. The answers are on page 48, but no cheating until you've finished the quiz!

1. WHICH OF THESE PLAYERS PERFORMS PRE-GAME RITUALS, INCLUDING TOSSING 40 SUNFLOWER SEEDS INTO THE GRASS?
a) Clayton Kershaw
b) Carlos Correa
c) Aaron Judge

2. WHICH TEAM SIGNED CENTER FIELDER CHARLIE BLACKMON TO A SIX-YEAR $108 MILLION CONTRACT?
a) Colorado Rockies
b) Arizona Diamondbacks
c) Los Angeles Angels

3. WHO SIGNED A CONTRACT FOR $325 MILLION OVER 13 YEARS—THE RICHEST CONTRACT IN THE HISTORY OF SPORTS TEAMS?
a) J.D. Martinez
b) Giancarlo Stanton
c) Joey Votto

4. WHICH PLAYER PICKED UP A GOLD GLOVE FOR HIS FIRST FIVE MLB SEASONS?
a) Nolan Arenado
b) Paul Goldschmidt
c) Starling Marte

5. J.D. MARTINEZ WAS SNAPPED UP BY THE RED SOX IN FEBRUARY 2018 WITH A FIVE-YEAR CONTRACT WORTH HOW MUCH?
a) $99 million
b) $108 million
c) $110 million

6. WHICH THIRD BASEMAN IS ALSO AN AVID STORM TRACKER?
a) Manny Machado
b) Mike Trout
c) Adrian Beltré

7. WHICH SIX-TIME MLB ALL-STAR IS THE HIGHEST PAID ATHLETE FROM CANADA?
a) Joey Votto
b) Justin Morneau
c) James Paxton

8. PAUL GOLDSCHMIDT GRADUATED FROM UNIVERSITY IN 2013 WITH A BACHELOR DEGREE IN WHICH SUBJECT?
a) Management
b) Business
c) Communication

9. WHICH NATIONALS PLAYER PREVIOUSLY PLAYED FOR THE ARIZONA DIAMONDBACKS AND DETROIT TIGERS, AND IS A SIX-TIME ALL-STAR?
a) Bryce Harper
b) Max Scherzer
c) Sean Dolittle

10. WHICH PLAYER CHANGES HIS BAT DEPENDING ON WHETHER HE IS BATTING AGAINST A LEFT-HANDED OR RIGHT-HANDED PITCHER?
a) Matt Carpenter
b) Freddie Freeman
c) Albert Pujois

11. WHICH PLAYER RECORDED HIS 2,500TH STRIKEOUT IN MAY 2018?
   a) Justin Verlander
   b) Madison Bumgarner
   c) Max Scherzer

12. COREY "KLUBOT" KLUBER HAS EARNED HIS NICKNAME PLAYING IN WHICH POSITION?
   a) Left fielder
   b) Pitcher
   c) First baseman

13. LEGEND HAS IT THAT CARDINALS SUPERSTAR MARK MCGWIRE TOLD MANAGER TONY LA RUSSA "IT MIGHT BE ONE OF THE WORST MOVES OF YOUR CAREER" IF HE DIDN'T PROMOTE WHICH PLAYER?
   a) Albert Pujois
   b) Carlos Matinez
   c) José Martínez

14. WHICH STARTING PITCHER IS NICKNAMED "THE CONDOR"?
   a) Clayton Kershaw
   b) Justin Verlander
   c) Chris Sale

15. WHICH TEXAS RANGERS PLAYER IS A MEMBER OF THE 3,000 HIT CLUB?
   a) Adrian Beltré
   b) Joey Gallo
   c) Ronald Guzmán

16. WHO WAS THE YOUNGEST RED SOX PLAYER IN 49 YEARS TO HIT A GRAND SLAM IN 2014?
   a) Mookie Betts
   b) Xander Bogaerts
   c) Jackie Bradley Jr.

17. SPORTS ILLUSTRATED RANKED WHICH PLAYER NUMBER ONE IN MLB BEFORE THE 2018 SEASON?
   a) Mike Trout
   b) Paul Goldschmidt
   c) Jose Altuve

18. WHICH GIANTS PLAYER ACHIEVED AN INCREDIBLE WORLD SERIES ERA OF 0.250?
   a) Johnny Cueto
   b) Mark Melancon
   c) Madison Bumgarner

19. WHICH PLAYER CHANGED HIS NUMBER FROM 13 TO 8 WHEN HE JOINED THE LOS ANGELES DODGERS?
   a) Chris Taylor
   b) Manny Machado
   c) Walker Anthony Buehler

20. WHO BECAME THE FOURTH PLAYER IN THE PAST 25 YEARS TO SCORE A HOME RUN BEFORE THE AGE OF 21?
   a) Giancarlo Stanton
   b) Bryce Harper
   c) Mookie Betts

21. WHICH CLEVELAND INDIANS PLAYER HAS THE NICKNAMES "PAQUITO" AND "MR. SMILE"?
   a) Michael Brantley
   b) Brad Hand
   c) Francisco Lindor

22. AT 19 YEARS OLD, WHO BECAME THE YOUNGEST PLAYER TO WIN THE ARIZONA FALL LEAGUE MVP AWARD IN 2016?
   a) Ozzie Albies
   b) Gleyber Torres
   c) Austin Meadows

23. SHOHEI OHTANI HOLDS THE RECORD FOR THE FASTEST PITCH FOR A JAPANESE PLAYER—WHAT SPEED DID HE ACHIEVE?
   a) 102.5 mph
   b) 104 mph
   c) 101.5 mph

24. HOW OLD WAS VLADIMIR GUERRERO JR. WHEN HE WAS SIGNED BY THE TORONTO BLUE JAYS IN 2015?
   a) 18
   b) 16
   c) 17

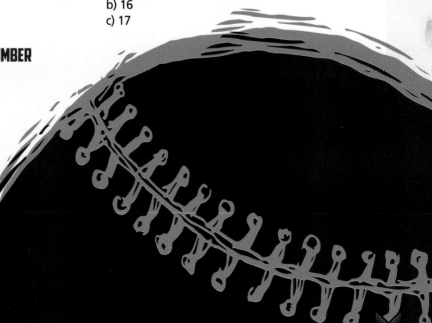

PICTURE CREDITS

The publishers would like to thank the following sources for their kind permission to reproduce the pictures in this book.

Getty Images: / Minas Panagiotakis: 36

REX/Shutterstock: /Elise Amendola/AP: 17; /Stephen Brashear/AP: 39B; /Paul Chiasson/AP: 37; Tony Dejak/AP: 10, 40, 45; /Jack Dempsey/AP: 22R; /David Dermer/AP: 23, 44; /Michael Dwyer/AP: 12; /Frank Franklin/AP: 32; /Ross D Franklin/AP: 39T; /Kyusung Gong/AP: 1; /Jae C Hong/AP: 25; /Bill Kostroun/AP: 11; /Kelvin Kuo/AP: 26; /Ben Margot/AP: 31L; /John Minchillo/AP: 19, 48; /Jim Mone/AP: 41; /Mike Nelson/EPA-EFE: 20; /Steve Nesius/AP: 22L; /Albert Pena/CSM: 21L, 27, 28; /David J Phillip/AP: 13, 31R, 42; /Gene J Puskar/AP: 18; / Richard W Rodriguez/AP: 33; /Rick Scuteri/AP: 8, 14, 21R, 43; /Eric Christian Smith/AP: 2; / Chris Szagola/CSM: 9; /Jason Szenes/EPA-EFE: 7; /Mark J Terrill/AP: 34, 35; /Shawn Thew/EPA-EFE: 4-5, 29; /Elaine Thompson/AP: 24; /Winslow Townson/AP: 16; /Nick Wass/AP: 6, 38; /Matt York/AP: 30; /David Zalubowski/AP: 15

Shutterstock: /Sanit Fuangnakhon: backgrounds

QUIZ ANSWERS

1. c	13. a
2. a	14. c
3. b	15. a
4. a	16. a
5. c	17. a
6. b	18. c
7. a	19. b
8. a	20. a
9. b	21. c
10. c	22. b
11. a	23. a
12. b	24. b